Made in the USA
Coppell, TX
19 May 2025

49574432R00052